CW00368859

1

Golfing Ephemera

About the Author

Sarah Baddiel is one of the world's leading dealers in golf books and ephemera. Her gallery in Grays Antique Market, London, draws collectors from all over the world and she has an extensive collection of her own. A frequent visitor to America, she is a member of both the United States Golf Association and the United States Golf Collectors Society. She has advised many golf clubs on their collections and is much in demand as a speaker. She is the author of several articles on golfiana and her book *Golf: the Golden Years*, published in 1989, was a bestseller.

Modes & Travaux

Costume de sport
en cloqué bleu
création de
MOLYNEUX

EDITIONS EDOUARD BOUCHERIT

France et Colonies : 4 francs

10, Rue de la Pépinière, Paris

*Magazine covers such as this French one from the 1930s are some
of the most pleasing items of golfing ephemera*

Golfing Ephemera

SARAH FABIAN BADDIEL

CHAPMANS
1991

CHAPMANS LIBRARY OF GOLF

Editor Tim Jollands
Designer Humphrey Stone

Chapmans Publishers Ltd
141-143 Drury Lane
London WC2B 5TB

A CIP Catalogue record
for this book is available from
the British Library

ISBN 1 85592 553 2

First published by Chapmans in 1991
Copyright © Sarah Baddiel and
Jollands Editions 1991
Text copyright © Sarah Baddiel 1991
Photographs © Sarah Baddiel Collection 1991

Special photography by Bill Burnett

Text set in Palatino
Typeset by Character Graphics,
Taunton, Somerset
Printed in Spain for Imago

CONTENTS

Acknowledgements 7

Introduction 8

Advertising 10

Autographs and Letters 12

Blotters 14

Bookmarks 16

Bookplates 17

Calendars 18

Cigarette Cards 22

Comics 25

Greetings Cards 26

Magazines 28

Manufacturers' Catalogues 30

Matchbox Labels and Book Match Covers 31

Menus 32

Music Covers 34

Packaging 36

Pamphlets 38

Periodicals 40

Playing Cards and Games 42

Postage Stamps and Covers 44

Postcards 46

Posters 48

Programmes 50

Rule Books and Club Handbooks 52

Tickets 54

Tradecards 56

Travel Pamphlets and Luggage Lables 58

Victorian Scraps 60

Miscellany 61

Bibliography and Useful Addresses 62

ACKNOWLEDGEMENTS

WHEN Tim Jollands invited me to contribute the first book in the series Chapmans Library of Golf, little did he know what he was taking on. I can only thank him for his tremendous help, support and encouragement during the preparation of the book. On behalf of the two of us, I would also like to thank Stuart R. MacKenzie, editor of *Tee Time*, for his work on golf stamps; the production team of Humphrey Stone, Mark Curnock (Character Graphics) and Christine Hoy (Chapmans) for their unflappability when deadlines loomed; and Ian and Marjory Chapman for making it all possible in the first place.

I would like to dedicate the book to a very dear friend, Karen Elder, the 'Queen of Ephemera'. Sadly she died in March.

SARAH FABIAN BADDIEL
London, May 1991

[7]

INTRODUCTION

IN January 1991, a 20-page pamphlet entitled *Laws of Musselburgh Golf Club* was sold at auction for £29,700. It is the record price for a piece of golf literature and underlines the extraordinary growth in the collecting of golfiana over the last twenty years. Old clubs, paintings, ceramics, silverware and books – all prized by collectors – were made to last. This book concentrates on printed matter of a more ephemeral nature, of which the Musselburgh pamphlet might be considered the ultimate example.

The word 'ephemera' refers to something short-lived, 'here today gone tomorrow'. Attempts have been made over the years to define the term from the collecting point of view, notably by members of the Ephemera Society. In the first issue (November 1975) of their journal, *The Ephemerist*, they offered the following guideline: 'To the uninitiated the word is faintly suspect. To the initiate it may or may not cover a multitude of items, from cigarette cards to uniform buttons. To the Ephemera Society it has fairly precisely defined limits: it covers "printed or hand-written items produced specifically for short-term use and, generally, for disposal".' In the context of this book, I have kept to paper items but make no apologies for including borderline categories such as cigarette cards, magazines and periodicals, postcards and postage stamps.

Old scorecards recalling favourite rounds, the occasional tournament programme or admission ticket, last year's fixture list . . . there can hardly be a golfer in the land who is not already, to a certain extent, a collector of golfing ephemera. My own interest in the game began about fifteen years ago at a time when I was dealing in juvenile and illustrated books. This took me around the country in my search for stock and, purely for fun, I started to collect items of golfiana. Before long I was acquiring duplicate material which could be exchanged with the small circle of fellow collectors or sold alongside my main stock. The collection grew, as did the number of duplicates, and eventually golf took over. Since then, collecting and dealing in golfiana has been my full-time escapist hobby – and livelihood.

Collecting can be as frustrating as the game itself. The search has taken me to antiques centres, auction houses, car-boot sales, flea markets, golf clubs, junk shops, secondhand bookshops, specialist fairs and numerous private houses. Sometimes you return tired, despondent and empty handed. At other times a long-neglected suitcase of someone else's 'rubbish' will reveal a treasure. Important items do still turn up in the most unexpected places. An old chest of drawers had been sent to auction and, purely by chance, the drawers were removed prior to the sale. Out fell a small pamphlet, the 1763 edition of Thomas Mathison's famous poem *The Goff*, hidden perhaps for two hundred years. Fortunately the auctioneer realised its importance and it fetched a record price in a specialist golf auction.

The number of collectors has grown enormously in recent years, not only in Britain but also in the United States, Japan and Europe. During the 1980s prices soared as the collecting boom took off but, at the time of writing, the recession is biting hard and prices are returning to a more sensible level. Fortunately, golfing ephemera forms a vast area of collecting that suits all pockets.

The pleasure derived from rescuing the 300-odd items in this book has been immense. In sharing them with a wider audience, I hope existing collectors will recognise a few old friends and find inspiration in others. For those not yet stricken with the collecting bug, I hope this window on the past will, at least, provide an enjoyable interlude between rounds. And if it sends you scurrying to the attic, so much the better.

A New Hudson Bicycle is part of every good sportsman's equipment !

The Golfer

has considerable need of a dependable, hard-wearing Bicycle, always right and tight, ready for use any time, anywhere.

And like many another Sportsman, the Golfer finds many daily needs in his business for the faithful, unfailing service of a

NEW HUDSON

BICYCLE.

WE WOULD LIKE TO DEMONSTRATE TO YOU
NEW HUDSON VALUE AND DEPENDABILITY—Please Step Inside!

ADVERTISING

ADVERTISING is a continuous theme in this book. Since the 1890s, an obsession with golf on both sides of the Atlantic has been exploited to the full by companies trying to promote their products. The New Hudson Bicycle poster employs a delightful golfing image to lure the passer-by of the mid-1920s. Then it was up to the copywriter to persuade you to 'step inside'. Unrestricted by the Trades Descriptions Act, North British Rubber were able to make extravagant claims about their Kite and Hawk balls on the c1913 advertising cards below – and even Selfridges imply that they have the endorsement of the R&A.

The link between product and golf is often tenuous, stretching the skill of the copywriter to the limit: 'The Scotch lassie, like her English sister, revels in a game of Golf and does the course with zest, knowing that her Sphere Suspenders will keep her ever trim and neat.'

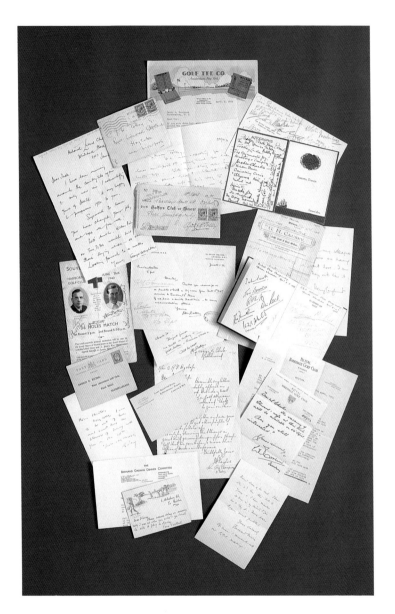

AUTOGRAPHS AND LETTERS

THE closest that one can get to the famous players of the past is through their autographed letters. There is something very special about handling a letter written by one of golf's household names, particularly when it throws new light on an aspect of the writer's career or personality. Such letters are prized by collectors, with a price to match. At the other end of the scale, the autographs of current stars can cost you nothing – and if you can persuade an Open champion to sign the official programme for the year in which he won, so much the better.

The autographed material opposite includes letters from J.H. Taylor and Henry Cotton as well as writers Bernard Darwin, Henry Longhurst and the 'poet laureate of golf', Andrew Lang. G.H. Causey's billhead for 1912 and the Golf Tee Company's letterhead (1933) are faithful to the style of their times and interesting documents in their own right. The receipt below has the added interest of being issued by the golf club that is generally acknowledged as being the oldest (1744) in the world.

No. 744

Honourable Company of Edinburgh Golfers.

Edinburgh, 189 5

Received from David Maitland Esq.

the sum of Three Pounds Three Shillings sterling, being his Subscription to the Honourable Company of Edinburgh Golfers for the year from 1st January 189 to 31st December 189.

£3, 3s.   Secretary.

BLOTTERS

IN the age of pen ank ink, blotter advertising provided an effective means of keeping your name in front of customers. Employing popular images of the day, blotters made attractive gifts and occasionally you will come across one with a golfing theme. It is remarkable that such ephemeral objects as those illustrated have managed to survive for more than fifty years.

The Sutton & Sons blotter of 1922 is of particular interest and must have been expensive to produce. It has a Bakelite cover and pegs to hold the sheets of blotting paper in place. The photographs in each corner show (top left) Joyce Wethered, winner of the Ladies' Amateur Championship at Prince's, Sandwich; (top right) Walter Hagen, winner of the Open Championship at Royal St George's, Sandwich; and action from (bottom left) the Scottish Amateur Championship at St Andrews and (bottom right) the Glasgow Herald 1000 Guineas Tournament at Gleneagles. Few of the negatives survive for early photographs so a blotter such as this becomes doubly important to the collector.

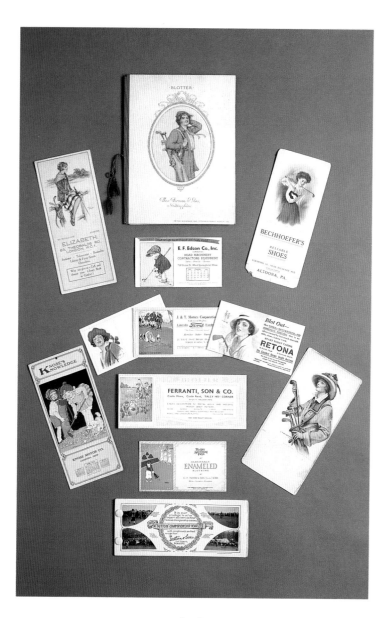

BOOKMARKS

THERE are not too many golf-related bookmarks but the very best are those issued by the Glasgow and South Western Railway around 1910. The set of four features (from left to right) James Braid, Tom Fernie, H.E. Taylor and E.B.H. Blackwell with profiles of the golfers on the back. Advertising, information and usefulness combine well in this simple ephemeral concept. These are originals, but the set has been reprinted recently so collectors should make sure they know what they are buying.

The oldest bookmarks in the group are the Libby's boy and girl, chromo-lithos probably produced during the golf boom of the 1890s. Ephemera is often difficult to date but there is no such problem with the bookmark issued to celebrate a gathering of the USA Golf Collectors Society in 1976.

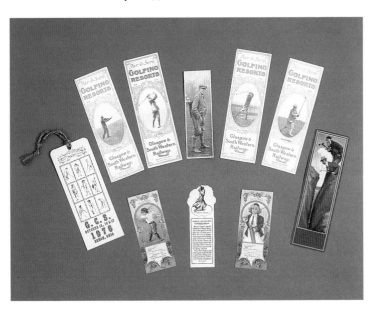

BOOKPLATES

Bookplates and book labels are usually found pasted into books but you do occasionally come across loose ones. Those with a golfing theme are few and far between and largely confined to golf clubs with extensive libraries, such as the R&A. I know of several collectors who have commissioned their own bookplates but Bobby Jones would appear to be the only household name to have had one.

CALENDARS

GOLF has been the subject of numerous calendars, the vast majority of which are promotional. Unlike much ephemera it is possible to date them precisely, the earliest of those shown opposite (bottom left) being the calendar for 1901 issued by William C. Haury of Collinsville, Connecticut. The most recent (1978) calendar in the group (top centre) features one of golf's most famous images, William Nicholson's woodblock illustration for the month of October from *An Almanack of Twelve Sports*, first published in 1897.

For the collector, the most sought-after calendars are those published for the Life Association of Scotland between 1892 and 1916. The quality of the illustrations, which covered famous players, championships and matches of the period, is superb. All but two are almost certainly the work of the Edinburgh painter, J. Michael Brown, but it must be said that those for 1908 and 1909 are out of character. The original watercolours remain in private hands but similar paintings by him would reach about £10,000 at auction. Few of the calendars have survived intact and those in excellent condition might fetch between £450 and £1000. The following is a checklist of the 25 scenes depicted:

1892 St Andrews from the Links (by J.H. Blair) *colour*
1893 North Berwick (by J.H. Blair) *colour*
1894 Playing to the Briars, Hoylake: John Ball, Harold Hilton, Johnny Laidlay, Leslie M. Balfour-Melville *colour*
1895 Amateurs v Professionals at Royal St George's, 1894
1896 Amateur Golf Championship at St Andrews, 1895: Leslie M. Balfour-Melville v John Ball
1897 Parliamentary Golf Handicap at Tooting Bec, 1896
1898 Ladies' Championship at Gullane, 1897
1899 Match at Duddingston, 1898: Freddie Tait and Leslie M. Balfour-Melville v Willie Auchterlonie and Ben Sayers
1900 Match at Byfleet, 1899: Horace Hutchinson v Mure Fergusson
1901 Amateur Championship at Sandwich, 1900: J. Robb v Harold Hilton
1902 Ladies' Championship at Aberdovey, 1901: Molly Graham v Rhona Adair
1903 First International Golf Match, England v Scotland, at Hoylake, 1902

*A delightful chromo-litho advertising calendar for 1910, the actual
calendar having being removed*

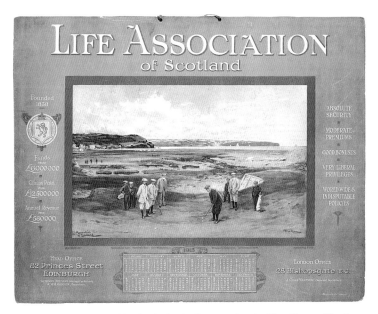

*The Life Association of Scotland calendar for 1913, showing Hon. Osmund Scott,
Hon Denys Scott, Captain Molesworth, Horace Hutchinson and Captain Prideaux
Brune approaching the 4th hole at Westward Ho!*

1904 First International Professional Golf Match, England v Scotland, at
     Prestwick, 1903
1905 Amateur Championship at Sandwich, 1904
1906 Surviving Open Champions, St Andrews, 1905
1907 Surviving Amateur Champions, Hoylake, 1906
1908 Tom Morris, Professional of the Royal & Ancient GC
1909 Horace Hutchinson, Captain of the Royal & Ancient GC
1910 North Berwick Links, Perfection Bunker
1911 Punch Bowl Hole, Hoylake
1912 High Hole, St Andrews
1913 Westward Ho! *colour* (see illustration above)
1914 Royal County Down, 11th hole: the Rt Hon. The Earl Annesley, Col
     R.H. Wallace, Lionel O'Munn, H.E. Reade *colour*
1915 Prestwick, Himalaya Hole: George Duncan, J.H. Taylor, James Braid,
     Harry Vardon *colour*
1916 Lloyd George at Walton Heath: with James Braid, Herbert W. Fowler
     and Lord Riddell *colour*

CIGARETTE CARDS

CIGARETTE cards were printed specifically to be collected in order to encourage brand loyalty amongst smokers. They were first produced in the United States in the late 1870s and they became so popular that Allen & Ginter introduced them to Britain in 1884. British companies were soon issuing them in vast quantities on a broad range of popular subjects as the collecting bug swept through the land.

Few records survive so dating is difficult but the first cards with a golfing theme were issued c1897 by Cope Brothers and Ogden's. Cope's commissioned 'George Pipeshank' (J. Wallace), who had illustrated two small posters for them in 1893, to paint 50 subjects for their Cope's Golfers series. The watercolours, painted actual size, have survived and are in private hands. A set of the chromo-litho reproductions fetches about £2500; most of us have to settle for the Nostalgia reprints (see overleaf).

As part of the 'tobacco war', Ogden's issued between 1897 and 1907 some 27,000 different photographic cards under their Guinea Gold and Tabs series, amongst which were subsets on golfers. These included cards featuring, respectively, Tom Morris and John Ball (see opposite). Few other golfing sets were issued until the heyday of card issues in the 1920s and 1930s and most of the cards illustrated come from this era. Churchman's catered well for the golfer and one of my favourite sets is their Prominent Golfers, featuring caricatures by 'Mel' of the likes of Walter Hagen and Abe Mitchell (see opposite). The map of Prestwick – venue for so many of the early Open Championships – is in the format adopted for larger packs. They were not so easy to store or use as 'flick' cards but are very popular today.

Insert cards have appeared in a vast range of products and occasionally you come across one with a golfing theme. I have included some with the cigarette cards, pride of place going to Bobby Jones, Gene Sarazen and Walter Hagen.

GOLF CIGARETTE CARDS – KNOWN SETS

Felix Berlyn, Manchester				
Humorous Golfing Series				
Small size	25	c1910	a1	C
Postcard size (139 x 87mm)	25	c1910		D
W.A. & A.C. Churchman, Ipswich				
Famous Golfers	50	1927	a	D
Famous Golfers				
1st series	12	1927	b	B
2nd series	12	1928	b	B
Prominent Golfers	50	1931	a	D
Prominent Golfers	12	1931	b	B
Three Jovial Golfers in Search				
of the Perfect Golf Course				
English issue	36	1934	a	A
Irish issue	72	1934	a	D
Can You Beat Bogey at St Andrews?				
1st edition	55	1934	a	A
2nd edition	58	1934	a	A
Wm Clarke & Son, Dublin				
Golf Terms (subset; 38 x 58mm)	12	1900		E
Cope Bros & Co. Ltd, Liverpool				
Cope's Golfers				
Wide card	50	1897	a	G
Narrow card	50	1897	a	G
Golf Strokes (70 x 45mm)	32	1923		D
John Cotton Ltd, Edinburgh				
Golf Strokes				
A & B	50	1936	a1	D
C & D	50	1937	a1	E
E & F	50	1938	a1	E
G & H	50	1939	a1	G
I & J	50	1939	a1	G
W. & F. Faulkner				
Golf Terms	12	1901	d2	F
Imperial Tobacco, Canada				
How to Play Golf	50	1925	a	C
Smokers Golf Cards	127	1926	a	E
Marsuma Ltd, Congleton				
Famous Golfers and their Strokes	50	1914	a	F
Mecca Cigarettes, New York				
Champion Golfers (60 x 75mm)	6	1930		B
J. Millhoff & Co Ltd, London				
Famous Golfers	27	1928	a2	C
Morris & Sons Ltd, London				
Golf Strokes	25	1923	d	A
Ogden's Ltd, Liverpool				
Guinea Gold subset	18	c1901	d	D
Tabs subset	15	c1901	d	E
John Player & Sons, Nottingham				
Championship Golf Courses	25	1936	b	B
Golf (various issues)	25	1939	b	B
W.D. & H.O. Wills, Bristol				
Golfing	25	1924	b	B
Famous Golfers	25	1930	b	D

Dimensions a 36 x 68mm, b 62 x 80mm, d 37 x 62mm
(1 slightly larger, 2 slightly smaller).
Values A £50-100, B £100-150, C £150-200, D £200-300,
E £300-500, F £500-1000, G over £1000.

29.—The " Mashie."

9.—Andrew Lang.
" The Laureate of Golf."

The table opposite shows the golfing sets known to have been issued up to the Second World War, which effectively ended the production of cigarette cards. The values are for sets in mint condition. Condition does matter and the prices will drop dramatically for creased or damaged cards. If buying singly, expect to pay up to three times as much for the end cards in a series – they were the first to get damaged or lost. These sets, plus the many other cards which appear in sporting and general sets, form a wonderful source of reference – both visual and written – for the early days of the game.

COMICS

CHILDREN's comics should not be overlooked for the golf stories as well as their excellent artwork. As comics were handed around from one child to another it is hard to find them in good condition. This is a case of finding what you can and then hoping to improve upon it at a later date.

GREETINGS CARDS

I have a great weakness for greetings cards, particularly those of the sentimental and romantic variety so popular during the period 1905 to 1920. They combine elegance and ingenuity and some of them are worth collecting just for the verses:

> In the links of friendship
> I send this wish,
> Hoping it will suit you
>   To a tee

Early greetings cards are not so easy to find as postcards and are therefore rather more expensive. Fortunately, the standard of modern cards has risen appreciably in recent years and there are some excellent examples to be found.

MAGAZINES

Many of the popular magazines of the early years of this century had images of golf on their front covers yet no golf content inside, a sure reflection of the game's drawing power. American magazines such as *The Ladies' Home Journal*, *Collier's* and *The Saturday Evening Post* had many collectable covers, some of them by illustrators like Norman Rockwell, which can be found mounted and framed at prices up to £100. The temptation to 'break' these magazines if complete should be avoided at all costs.

One of the earliest magazines to feature golf on the front cover is *The Illustrated American* of 25 August 1894. It is rare and complete would set you back about £60, but well worth it for Aubrey Beardsley's classic depiction of golf in the Gay Nineties. (It had been used that June on an invitation to the opening of Prince's Ladies Golf Club in England.) The decade saw a phenomenal growth of interest in the game in America, from only a handful of golf courses in 1890 to close on a thousand in 1900.

MANUFACTURERS' CATALOGUES

Catalogues issued by manufacturers and retailers of golf equipment offer a means of identifying and dating clubs, balls and the many other artefacts associated with the game, ranging from tees to trolleys. This makes them of particular interest to specialists searching for background information on items in their collections. For collectors with a less specific purpose in mind, the catalogues featuring equipment made under licence of a well known champion are the most sought after. Few early catalogues have survived, which is not surprising as the natural reaction on receipt of a new catalogue is to throw away the out-of-date one. Those illustrated are from the 1920s to 1950s. The 1921 Dunlop catalogue is decorated throughout in a style that owes much to Art Deco and is a collector's item in its own right. That it is about golf only adds to its charm for me.

MATCHBOX LABELS
AND BOOK MATCH COVERS

Pictorial matchbox labels date back to 1830, since when hundreds of thousands of different designs have been used by manufacturers vying for the attention of the smoker. The oldest of those shown below is the yellow Golf label, just below the delightful cigar label. Labels are difficult to date but after 5 April 1916 all matchboxes sold in Britain had to display a contents figure, as in the Caddy label. The Ohio Blue Tip label is a 'skillet', the design being printed directly onto the box's cardboard cover.

Invented in 1899, book matches have been a phenomenally successful means of cheap advertising and in America alone about a million of them are handed out *each hour*. Those with a golfing theme can be highly decorative and some even double up as scorecards. My own favourite is the one which exhorts golfers to 'Win your match with the matchless Click Colonel Golf Balls. Eclipse all others with Flight, Endurance, Accuracy.'

MENUS

Aɴɴᴜᴀʟ dinners have inspired numerous menus with a golfing theme, ranging from the delightful Diner de la Saint-Martin (1919) to Roy Ullyett's treatment for the Association of Golf Writers' dinner 70 years later. Menus are scarce, which makes the 1925 menu for Royal Blackheath, the oldest club in England, a prized item. The menu card issued by Guinness carries the following advice:

> If you foozle with your cleek,
> And your putts are – let's say –
>   rather weak;
> If your drives, for all to see,
> Do not always leave the tee,
> And to slice them is a habbit –
> If, in short, you are a rabbit,
> Do not put your clubs away –
> Drink a Guinness every day.
> *(Guinness is, we'd like to add,*
> *Good for those who aren't so bad.)*

MUSIC COVERS

PRIOR to radio and television, households would gather round the piano for entertainment and the majority of golf songs come from this era. To my knowledge there are about fifty sheet music covers with a golfing theme, the songs seldom living up to the quality of the artwork. This from 'Tee High! Tee Low!' (1928):

When you play a game of golf through to eighteen
You need a bag of clubs with shafts strong and lean
Have a nice white ball
And a caddie to run up
To hand out the putter to roll into the cup
Set up the flag, before the call of fore
Clear the green, then mark your score . . .

Although it cannot be termed ephemera, I have included opposite *The Golf Song Book* (1903). Edited by John Kerr, best known for his *Golf Book of East Lothian*, and featuring a painting by Michael Brown on its cover, it commands up to £1200 at auction.

PACKAGING

UP to now I have considered only two-dimensional items but the three-dimensional area of packaging is truly ephemeral. Many of the golf ball boxes opposite look fairly tatty but amongst collectors of golf balls – the fastest-growing field in golfiana – such items are now highly valued. Silvertown are reckoned to have issued the first golf ball box *c*1895 and their rivals soon followed suit. The most sought-after boxes are those produced up to 1930, a period which saw the gutta-percha ball being replaced by the rubber-core 'Haskell' and manufacturers producing a wonderful array of outer casings in their search for the ideal golf ball. By 1930 the dimple pattern had become the norm. Of those illustrated, the White Colonel (*c*1910) and North British (*c*1912) boxes are particularly fine examples of the art of packaging.

The wooden and plastic tee pegs that we know today were introduced between the wars, prior to which most golfers relied on a pinch of dampened sand. Moulds were developed for shaping the sand and the Spurgin Manufacturing Company of Chicago were able to offer a booklet of Novel-Tees which 'can the sand': you tore off the stiffened paper, shaped it between the fingers and filled it with sand. For the less dextrous, Colonel Bogey's Tee Cups – made of cardboard – presented a simpler solution. Also bearing the name of Colonel Bogey is the small round box of card tees which, like the others, were made prior to the First World War. It amazes me how they have managed to survive after all these years. Of the later items shown opposite, I particularly like the Diamond Company's combined match book and tee holder which, when opened, reveals a scorecard.

Tracking down such items of ephemera takes time and patience but the satisfaction in finding good examples is immense. Anyone looking for further inspiration is strongly advised to visit Robert Opie's magnificent museum of packaging at Gloucester. Note, however, that there are very few golfing items in his collection.

PAMPHLETS

GOLF has spawned a great miscellany of pamphlets. Some of them, like the Dexter catalogue (opposite), are of interest merely because they employ golf as a decorative motif; others have more substance. Anything connected with golf-course architecture has a ready market these days. Martin Sutton's *The Layout and Upkeep of Golf Courses and Putting Greens* is in fact an offprint from his excellent *Book of the Links*, published in 1912. For a sixth of the price, the pamphlet provided greenkeepers with all the essential information and it makes fascinating reading today. Of even greater relevance today is the Audubon Societies' publication, *Golf Clubs as Bird Sanctuaries*.

The Silvertown Company's four-page pamphlet is particularly collectable as it is connected with the Open Championship; Royal Lytham and St Annes; Bobby Jones, the winner; and the history of the golf ball. Its advertisements for golf balls include one for the Silver King 'Black Recess', thus enabling one to put a date of *c*1926 to the pack of playing cards on page 42.

OPEN CHAMPIONSHIP
1926
ROYAL LYTHAM and ST ANNE'S
JUNE 23—24—25

With the Compliments of
THE SILVERTOWN COMPANY
106 CANNON ST., LONDON, E.C.4.

PERIODICALS

THE first golf periodical – *Golf: A Weekly Record of 'Ye Royal and Ancient Game'* – appeared in Britain in 1890 and has continued to the present day under the title *Golf Illustrated*, which it adopted in 1899. America followed suit with *The Golfer* (1894 to 1903) and many others sprang up on both sides of the Atlantic in response to the golf boom at the turn of the century. By the 1930s golfers were spoilt for choice.

Early periodicals are a prime source of reference for collector and historian alike. They can be enjoyed on many levels, ranging from their often decorative covers and wealth of illustration to long-forgotten articles by and about the leading figures of the day. To the collector, advertisements often provide the answer when trying to date golf balls and other items of equipment.

Of those shown opposite, *Golfing* (the lower of the two bearing that title) enjoyed a continuous run from 1898 before being combined in 1970 into *Golf World*, Britain's leading periodical of today. The longest surviving is *Golf Monthly* (1910 to date), edited in its formative years by Harold Hilton – the two issues featured come from the year in which he won both the British and US Amateur Championships. In 1900 and 1901 he had won back-to-back British Amateur titles, a feat matched in the US Amateur during the very same years by Walter Travis, editor until 1920 of *The American Golfer* (1908 to 1936). Travis was succeeded by Grantland Rice, one of the world's best-known sports writers. The Chicago-based *Golfers Magazine* (1902 to 1931), famous for its fine covers, was edited by another champion turned writer, Chick Evans. *Golf* (1897 to 1917) and the American *Golf Illustrated* (1914 to 1935) were other quality publications of the day.

Count yourself lucky if you have inherited a bound volume or two of *Golf Illustrated* as 50 early volumes fetched £42,000 at auction in 1990. For the rest of us it is a matter of searching hard for the occasional stray issue.

PLAYING CARDS AND GAMES

ALTHOUGH card games were introduced to the English court as early as 1488, it was not until the Victorian era that playing cards were mass produced. They formed an integral part of indoor entertainment prior to the advent of televison and even today there can hardly be a household without a pack of cards.

Given the popularity of golf during the early part of this century, it is not surprising that manufacturers of playing cards produced packs designed to appeal to the golfer. Illustrated opposite are some of those collected over the years. Ideally one should try to collect complete sets in fine condition and in their original wrapping. So saying, I have never turned down the opportunity to acquire a stray card if it has a pleasing golf motif on it.

The concertina wallet at the top of the page is particularly interesting as it provides unwitting evidence of America's first golf boom. In 1895 there were under a hundred golf courses in the United States: such was the national obsession with the game some ten years later that the American Playing Card Company was able to equip its salesmen with samples of 25 different designs. Such confidence in the market would be unthinkable today, despite golf's huge following worldwide.

Playing cards offered a good medium for advertising. The distinctive way in which the St Mungo Manufacturing Company promoted and packaged their 'Colonel' range of golf balls is in evidence again, while the cards issued by Sinclair's of Newcastle to promote Foursome Tobacco are in the same style as their tobacco tins and the cigarette pack on page 31.

One of the earliest card games devoted to golf is Card Golf. The set comprising 60 chromo-litho cards depicting Drive (6), Stroke (24), Obstacle (12), The Approach (6), On the Green (6) and Hole (6) was printed in Bavaria c1895. The complicated rules may account for the good condition in which it has remained – a set without its rules and box realised £220 at Phillips in 1990.

POSTAGE STAMPS AND COVERS

THE first stamp with a golfing connection – albeit tenuous – was a view of Mt Unzen from Japan's Sasebo golf course. Cape Verde was the first to depict an actual golfer in 1962, since when there has been a steady output of stamps throughout the world, particularly in the Caribbean. Of particular interest is the stamp and set of five covers issued to commemorate the fiftieth anniversary of Bobby Jones's Grand Slam and subsequent retirement. Gary Player, Babe Zaharias, Francis Ouimet and Harry Vardon are other players to have been depicted on stamps, the latter in connection with Royal Jersey's centenary issue.

The golf-related stamps listed below are accompanied by their Stanley Gibbons catalogue numbers – where listed – and many of them are illustrated in the Olmans' *Encyclopedia of Golf Collectibles*.

Alderney 1983 (A1, A11); Australia 1974 (573); Bahamas 1968 (315); Bermuda 1971 (279-82); Bhutan 1984 (590); Bophuthatswama 1980 (64-5); Cape Verde 1962 (389); Cayman Islands 1987 (647); China 1986 (3475); Christmas Island 1980 (120-1), 1986 (225); Cocos Keeling 1987 (164); Colombia 1980 (1544); Cook Islands 1969 (303), 1985 (1044); Dominican Republic 1957 (675, 686), 1959 (791), 1974 (1202-5); Ecuador 1975 (1591); France 1962 (1550), 1980 (2377); French Polynesia 1971 (138), 1974 (177-8); French West Africa 1958 (103); Gambia 1976 (346-8); Greece 1979 (1487); Grenada 1976 (773), 1979 (1029); Guernsey 1985 (315); Indonesia 1977 (1477); Ireland 1975 (373-4); Italy 1988 (1996); Jamaica 1979 (462), 1983 (462a), 1986 (652); Jersey 1978 (183-6), 1989 (470); Japan 1953 (719); Luxembourg 1980 (643); Maldive Islands 1990 (1392); Montserrat 1967 (193), 1970 (262), 1986 (711); Morocco 1974 (382); Nauru 1984 (306); New Caledonia 1987 (819), 1988 (822); Nicaragua 1963 (1497); Norfolk Island 1986 (391); Philippines 1988 (2095); Ras al Khaima 1971 (appendix); Redonda 1990; St Kitts-Nevis 1975 (342-5), 1978 (401), 1980 (04), 1988 (259); St Vincent 1975 (452); Samoa 1983 (645); Sharjah 1972 (appendix); Singapore 1981 (404); South Africa 1976 (396), 1979 (466); Sri Lanka 1989 (1097-8); Tanzania 1989 (658-9); Tonga 1990 (1109); Tunisia 1979 (925); United States 1981 (1906-7), 1988 (2356).

Also of interest to the collector in this relatively new and inexpensive field are the commemorative covers marking events such as the Open Championship and the US Masters.

[44]

POSTCARDS

AT the beginning of the century postcards offered the cheapest and most efficient means of communication and during the heyday of the picture postcard, 1902 to 1918, several million cards were sent through the post each day. Picture postcards were first sanctioned by the Post Office in 1894 but in 1902 the 'divided back' was introduced, allowing a message as well as the address to be written on the back. Until then, messages could only appear on the front. After the Great War, an increasing reliance on the telephone and the doubling, then trebling of postage contributed to the decline of the industry.

The golden age of the picture postcard coincided with golf's boom in popularity and this resulted in a prodigious output of golf cards, the leaders in the field being Raphael Tuck and Valentine's. I collect those that I like but many collectors concentrate on certain themes. Views of golf courses (perhaps those they have played, or championship courses, or even those that no longer exist) offer a fascinating record of how courses and clubhouses have evolved. Cards depicting the great golfers of the day are particularly popular and it is worth looking out for those published by Valentine's on the Open and Amateur Championships of 1902 onwards. Others prefer the humorous side of golf, collecting the work of well known artists like 'Bonzo', Tom Browne, 'Cynicus', Harry Furniss, Charles Dana Gibson, Phil May, Lance Thackeray and Lawson Woods. The scope is endless and one of the added joys of collecting postcards is that they so often provide a stamp, a postmark and a message on the back.

Prices vary enormously but a good collection can be built for about £5 a card. The hobby is served by *Picture Postcard Monthly* and *Collect Modern Cards* and the largest postcard fair – the 'Bloomsbury' – is held monthly (usually on the last Sunday) in London at the Royal National Hotel, Russell Square. Allow enough time to visit about 120 stands.

BY ROWLAND HILDER

Come to Britain
for GOLF

Published by the Travel Association of Great Britain and Northern Ireland (Tourist Division of the British Tourist and Holidays Board) and printed in Great Britain by W. S. Cowell Ltd. London & Ipswich.

POSTERS

THE expansion of the railways and spread of tourism has fostered a wonderful variety of colourful posters exhorting people to travel. Golf features frequently and I can think of few more effective posters than 'Come to Britain for Golf' (1950), with its striking Rowland Hilder painting and simple slogan. The young lady welcoming you to 'The Line to the Links' on the Seaboard poster (c1910) features elsewhere in Earl Christy's work.

Early golf posters are scarce. Limited numbers were printed and most of these were then pasted onto hoardings. Few survived once they had outlived their use. Those that have can reach astronomical prices at auction – a pre-First World War Caledonian Railways poster would set you back more than £3000.

PROGRAMMES

PROGRAMMES are highly collectable, particularly those from major events. The order of play for the third round of the 1926 Open is an important item for Bobby Jones collectors, added interest being provided by photographs, a map of the course and advertisements, some featuring golf balls – Cochrane's Two-Five, the Mesh Harlequin, the Silver King, Blue Dunlop Maxfli and a double-page spread showing the Mesh and Dimple patterns.

Official programmes put out by the USGA have, for a long time, been fairly lavish productions. The one produced for the 1955 US Open runs to more than a hundred pages and positively dwarfs the R&A's programme for the 1952 Open. Such restraint was cast aside in 1971 to mark the 100th Open. The painting on the front cover is of Willie Park, the first Open champion, whose grand-daughters allowed it to be reproduced for the first time.

The name of Park is synonymous with Musselburgh. The programme for the opening of their new course at Monktonhall is rare indeed as the club do not have a copy in their own archives.

RULE BOOKS
AND CLUB HANDBOOKS

THE ever-changing rules of golf have resulted in an enormous output of rule books and aids to interpretation from golf clubs and organisations as well as equipment manufacturers and retailers. Early examples provide some of the most pleasing items of golfing ephemera, the most sought after being those connected with major clubs such as the R&A. Several of those illustrated originate in the 19th century but if I was pressed to choose a favourite it would have to be the Dunlop Rubber Company's *Golf Penalties and Etiquette* (1920) which is illustrated throughout by Harry Rountree.

The club handbooks below are also of interest. Nearly all of them were produced by the Golf Clubs Association between the 1920s and 1950s. Bernard Darwin wrote about fifty and Robert Browning over three hundred!

[54]

TICKETS

GOLFING tickets and badges are truly ephemeral as they are so often lost or thrown away after the event. I would find it impossible to part with my own because of the memories they stir in me and I am always on the look out for others. Those for the US Masters are particularly hard to find and I count myself very fortunate to have come across the 1982 parking permit.

One of my favourite tickets is the Golfers Railway Ticket, issued by the North Eastern Railway Company in the 1890s. They were filled in by club secretaries and allowed members to travel first class at up to half price as long as they were used 'for the sole purpose of playing Golf'. This one is unused – how wonderful it would be to find a completed ticket for one of the great professionals!

The tickets below are delightful examples of the skill of the jobbing printer and have the added interest of providing documentary evidence of the opening of Selby's golf course.

TRADECARDS

PRINTED cards bearing the name, trade and address of an individual or company were some of the earliest forms of advertising. With the advent of chromolithography, the tradecard blossomed. Customers were treated to a feast of colourful images by traders anxious to promote their products or services. The more appealing the image, the more likely it was that the customer would retain the card and use the product again. Local stores would periodically change their designs while food manufacturers such as Cadbury's, Huntley & Palmers and – notably – the Leibig Extract of Meat Company (of Oxo fame) were to issue vast numbers in sets.

The lady golfer employed to promote Humphreys' Witch Hazel Oil (c1903) is the work of Maude Humphrey, a well known children's book illustrator who was also the mother of Humphrey Bogart. The theme of the lady golfer is continued below. Many of these cards come from America where – in marked contrast to Great Britain – women were welcomed at golf clubs at the turn of the century.

TRAVEL PAMPHLETS
AND LUGGAGE LABELS

Tourism and golf have been inextricably linked since before the First World War, the one feeding off the other. Pamphlets and brochures issued by tourist organisations, railway and shipping companies, airlines and hotels and the ephemera connected with the journeys themselves provide a happy hunting ground for the collector.

All of the items illustrated are drawn from the 1920s to 1950s and they include examples from France, Hawaii, Italy, Japan, South Africa, Switzerland and the West Indies as well as Great Britain and the United States. I am particularly fond of the 1930s luggage label for Deauville's Hotel du Golf. Most of the pamphlets have instantly appealing covers and there is always some snippet of information to be gleaned from the contents. In the case of *Golfing in Ulster*, a delightful 100-page booklet published by the Ulster Tourist

Development Association in 1949, we are treated to many photographs and detailed course descriptions for the 60 golf clubs in Ulster at the time. It is hard to believe that a day's golf could be played at Royal Portrush for five shillings; today it would cost you one hundred times that amount.

VICTORIAN SCRAPS

THE Victorian hobby of cutting out various paper oddments and pasting them in albums became a cult with the introduction of 'scraps' designed for the purpose. The combination of chromolithography (which in the 1860s and 1870s had brought the excitement of colour to an era used to monochrome printing), die-cutting and embossing gave them an immediate appeal and they were imported from Germany in huge quantities. From the 1890s, most of those sold in Britain were printed by Raphael Tuck. Of those below, the cat (c1910) and the scarce Spalding advertisement (c1908) were probably issued singly, whereas the others (c1890) would have been joined together by tabs and sold as a set. Scraps were also used to decorate firescreens and the folding, draught-excluding screens so popular at the turn of the century.

MISCELLANY

ILLUSTRATED below are a few examples of golfing ephemera that did not quite fit into a category elsewhere. They range in date from 1900 to 1990 and all of them have something of interest to the collector. The pin book, button cards and hooks-and-eyes reveal how far the golfing motif has extended. The hairnet envelope is one of the most unusual items that I have come across. Its link with golf is explained in the caption. Asked 'What have you got there?', the gentleman on the right replies: 'Some good hair nets my wife asked me to get so that she could play golf without a confounded hat on!' The persimmon seed, with its slogan 'Grow your own golf clubs', is a delightful piece of nonsense appealing to those in search of a stocking-filler for the golfer in their life. Items such as these add greatly to the fun of collecting.

BIBLIOGRAPHY
AND USEFUL ADDRESSES

SELECT BIBLIOGRAPHY

Cigarette Card Values. Murray Cards (International). 1991

Lewis, John. *Printed Ephemera*. W. S. Cowell, 1962; Antique Collectors Club,
   distributed by Faber & Faber, 1988

London Cigarette Card Company. *The Complete Catalogue of British Cigarette Cards*. Webb & Bower, 1982

Olman, John M. and Morton W. *The Encyclopedia of Golf Collectibles*. Books Americana, Alabama, USA, 1985

Rendell, Joan. *The Match, the Box and the Label*. David & Charles, 1983

Rickards, Maurice. *Collecting Printed Ephemera*. Phaidon Christie's, 1988

Serpell, Tom. *Golf on Old Picture Postcards*. Reflections of a Bygone Age, Keyworth, Nottingham, 1988

AUCTION HOUSES

Christie's (Scotland) Ltd
164-166 Bath Street, Glasgow G2 4TG (041 332 8134)

Phillips
New House, 150 Christleton Road, Chester, Cheshire CH3 5TD (0244 313936)

Sotheby's
34-35 New Bond Street, London W1A 2AA (071-493 8080)

Sporting Antiquities
47 Leonard Road, Melrose, Mass. 02176, USA (0101-617 662 6588)

GOLF MUSEUMS

Archie Baird's Golf Museum
Gullane Golf Club, Gullane, East Lothian (087 57277)

British Golf Museum
St Andrews, Fife KY16 9JD (0334 73423)

United States Golf Association
Golf House, Far Hills, NJ 07931, USA (0101-908 234 2300)

SHOPS AND DEALERS

Sarah Baddiel
Golf Gallery, Grays in the Mews B10, Davies Mews, London W1Y 1AR
 (071-408 1239)

David Berkowitz
Golf's Golden Years, 2929 N. Western Avenue, Chicago, Ill. 60618, USA
 (0101-708 934 4108)

London Cigarette Card Company
Sutton Road, Somerton, Somerset TA11 6QP (0458 73452)

McEwan Fine Books
Ballater, Aberdeenshire AB3 5UB (0338 554329)

Bob Pringle
49 Ayr Street, Troon, Ayrshire KA10 6EB (0292 311822)

SOCIETIES

Ephemera Society
12 Fitzroy Square, London W1P 5HQ

Ephemera Society of America
PO Box 10, Scohaire, NY 12157, USA

Golf Collectors Society
PO Box 491, Shawnee Mission, KS 66201, USA

[63]

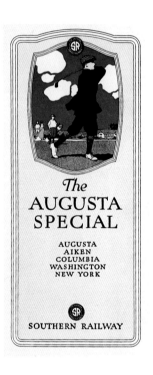

The
AUGUSTA
SPECIAL

**AUGUSTA
AIKEN
COLUMBIA
WASHINGTON
NEW YORK**

SOUTHERN RAILWAY